THE BASEMENT

True Crime Case of Serial Killer

Gary Heidnik

by: RJ PARKER

D1452544

THE BASEMENT

True Crime Case of Serial Killer
Gary Heidnik

by: RJ PARKER

ISBN-13: 978-1987902136
ISBN-10:   1987902130

Copyrights

Table of Contents

"This is a work of nonfiction. No names have been changed, no characters invented, no events fabricated."

– RJ Parker, PhD

More True Crime Books in the Kindle Store:

rjpp.ca/RJ-PARKER-BOOKS

The Early Life of Gary Heidnik

    Michael and Ellen Heidnik lived in a small Eastlake suburb of Cleveland, Ohio. They were a happy couple that lived in a small house in a friendly neighborhood. The neighbors never had any complaints from the couple. In November 1943, Ellen gave birth to a little boy, whom the two named Gary Michael Heidnik. A year later, they conceived another child, a son they named Terry.

Marital problems soon began to occur in the family, and by 1946, just three years after Gary's birth, Michael and Ellen divorced. The mother, Ellen, assumed custody of Gary and Terry for the next four years.

However, when Michael remarried, the two boys moved in with their father and his second wife. Later on, Heidnik claimed that he had been on the receiving end of severe emotional abuse from his father. He received a lot of taunts from him about his habits. For instance, his father would often humiliate him publicly when the family would go out. According to Gary, at one point, they were walking in a supermarket when he accidentally stumbled and fell in an aisle, knocking over a few items from the shelf. His dad picked him up and thrashed him so hard that the onlookers had to stop him.

Nocturnal enuresis (bedwetting) is a common trait of many serial killers. It isn't a psychological or physical illness but a developmental delay. Gary suffered with this as a child and adult. Numerous experts have talked about bedwetting being a problem in a child's early years. This usually stems from a lack of confidence and excessive fear, since they are scared and emotionally scarred. In most cases, parents are unable to handle the problem with patience and often resort to shaming and making fun of their child.

This just exacerbates the issue even further, since it makes the child more conscious of his actions. Unfortunately for Heidnik, he was never really able to control his bladder all his life. He later said that it was because of the emotional and mental trauma that he suffered as a child, which stuck to him every night he fell asleep in his bed.

Heidnik's father would make him hang up his stained sheets in his bedroom windows, in full view of his neighbors. It was one of the most embarrassing things that a father could do to his child. Many years later, when Gary was first arrested by the police and questioned about his childhood, he talked about the harrowing experiences he had had at the hands of his father. His father, Michael, denied the allegations, claiming that he had never abused his child.

The continuous mental torture that Gary had to face at home from his dad was one of the main reasons why he lacked confidence. He was always on the receiving end of taunts from his father, and this in turn led his stepmother to start abusing him. Gary later said that he found absolutely no peace at his home, and he would often keep himself confined in his room for most of the day.

As a result of the constant bickering and tensions at home, his confidence suffered drastically. In order to cope with his isolation, and as a defense mechanism, he developed fictional stories in his own head. He began to consider himself superior to his peers and colleagues, and decided that it "wasn't worth talking to them or needing their approval."

Gary completely stopped interacting with his fellow students, and it got to the point where he even stopped making eye contact with his teachers and other adults. Needless to say, he lost the few friends he had and became entirely isolated at school. When he was later arrested, Gary recalled an incident in class: a new female student once asked him about whether he had completed his homework that day or not. Rather than giving her a straight answer, Gary replied that she wasn't "worthy enough" to initiate a conversation with him.

One of Heidnik's most distinctive features was his oddly shaped head. It distinguished him from other kids, and he soon began to think of it as an object of pride. Gary and Terry believed that his head was shaped this way because he had fallen out of a tree as a child.

Despite being a social outcast, Heidnik was not stupid. In fact, he was one of the most intelligent students in his class, provided he decided to put his mind to something. He performed admirably in his academics, and tested out with an IQ of 130.

As he grew up, Heidnik's father started giving him advice and began to inspire him. Heidnik never forgave him, but he knew that he could benefit from his father's experience. At the age of 14, Heidnik's father asked him to change schools and encouraged him to join the Staunton Military Academy. It is now defunct but was located in Staunton, Virginia.

Off he went and joined the Academy and stayed there for two years, but he left just before his graduation. He then enrolled in a public high school and studied there until he turned 17. That's when he decided that he would join the United States Army and filled out the enrollment forms.

He was accepted into the Army and received basic training in combat over the next thirteen months. He was extremely dedicated and was highly focused. Heidnik excelled in most of the tasks and was described by his drill sergeant as "an excellent student." After his basic training was completed, Heidnik wanted to progress in the Army and applied for a variety of specialist positions, including the military police, but was unsuccessful. Following this, the Army gave him an opportunity to train as a medic. Heidnik accepted and was transferred to San Antonio, Texas. Again, he performed very well in medical training throughout his early days. Heidnik decided not to stay in San Antonio for an extended period of time and instead chose to transfer to the 46th Army Surgical Hospital in Landstuhl, West Germany. Just a few weeks after transferring to West Germany, he received his GED.

Heidnik was one of the best medics at the hospital, according to his colleagues, who often sang his praises. But just like back in school, Heidnik rarely talked with anyone, choosing to remain a social outcast, considering his peers and colleagues to be "beneath him." However, while he was able to excel and remain ahead of the pack back in school, the rejections from the military officers were still stuck in the back of his mind. Despite being a loyal servant of the United States Army, Heidnik later said that he never felt the pride or the distinguishing honor that his colleagues often talked about. He was just a man who was doing his job and nothing more.

At this point in time, Gary was not exhibiting any of the traits that other serial killers were known for. There was nothing distinguishing about his behavior or performance, and his colleagues simply thought that he was a man who liked to keep to himself. They never bothered him and he never bothered them. He did what he was told to do, and did it well.

Unfortunately, things began to change in the summer of 1962. In August, Heidnik reported to the hospital as a patient. He complained that he was suffering from a severe headache, mild dizziness and couldn't see properly. He was also experiencing severe nausea. Due to his headaches, a neurologist was called in to check up on his condition, hence ordering a battery of tests. Heidnik was initially diagnosed by the intake doctor with severe gastroenteritis. The neurologist, however, came up with a surprising find. According to his preliminary reports, Heidnik exhibited signs of mental illness. The neurologist prescribed him Stelazine (an antipsychotic drug used to treat anxiety and other psychotic disorders such as schizophrenia) in order to treat the condition.

Within two months of reporting sick in West Germany, Heidnik was transferred back to Philadelphia and admitted into a military hospital. The neurologist there who was overseeing him found that he was indeed suffering from a schizoid personality disorder. As a result of his mental condition, the Army gave him an honorable discharge and he mustered out.

It is not known whether or not Heidnik took the medication prescribed.

Post-Army Years

After he was released from military service, Heidnik continued to weigh out his options. What had promised to be a fantastic career in the military had suddenly been pulled short. The fact that the doctors said he was a "mental patient" further weighed on his mind.

Despite never showing it, Heidnik still considered himself to be "superior" as compared to others. This concept continued to form an important part of his thoughts, and he started developing a profound hatred for the military. Heidnik looked for jobs in the field of medicine after being released and eventually decided that he wanted to become a nurse.

He received his license soon after and began his career as a practical nurse in Philadelphia only. Simultaneously, Heidnik also decided that he would start attending school and enrolled at the University of Pennsylvania to study medicine. Heidnik's working years were not good; like many other individuals who later turned into heinous monsters, keeping a job was a major problem for him.

Heidnik's interest in medicine soon started to wane, and he dropped out of University after completing only one semester. He had started a new job as a psychiatric nurse at the Veterans Administration Hospital in Coatesville. This was a bad position for a man who thought himself to be superior to others. His experience as a psychiatric nurse was not good at all, primarily because he didn't know how to deal with mentally ill patients. According to his peers, Heidnik was often enraged when treating patients. Whereas nurses are trained to be very careful when dealing with mental patients, Heidnik didn't care at all. He was often seen scolding patients in private, and there were even reports of him manhandling certain patients. It wasn't long before the hospital decided that Heidnik's time was up and fired him. The reasons cited in the official report stated that Heidnik had very poor attendance and was also quite rude towards his patients.

From the money that he had acquired during his career, Heidnik was able to buy a three-story house near the Elwyn Institute, where he used to visit the mentally disabled. It's important to note that at this point in time, Heidnik did not have any physical contact with the opposite sex, something that was relatively common for a young man.

His lack of interaction with others was a major reason for this, since he didn't think there was anybody "worthy enough." While it may not seem so, this continued to weigh down on him and had a profound impact on his activities throughout his life. Heidnik's mother, Ellen, had completely let go of her life by this point. She had been hospitalized many times and had been diagnosed with bone cancer several years prior.

She had been found overdosing on medication and was suffering from alcoholism. Her condition continued to deteriorate until 1970. Her life was going downhill, and she had nothing to her name. Like many others who suffer from extreme depression and alcoholism, Ellen Heidnik eventually committed suicide. The cause of suicide was pretty obvious: she died by drinking mercuric chloride. During the autopsy, alcohol and several drugs were found in her system as well.

Even though he tried to wave it off, his mother's death left a huge impact on Heidnik's life. He was completely shattered and, compounded with the inability to hold a steady job or to have any sort of a social life, Heidnik decided that he had had enough of it.

This was the first of many suicide attempts that he made until his arrest. Just like his mother, Gary tried to overdose. Unfortunately, his attempt was unsuccessful, and he was found and taken to a hospital, where he recovered. Until his arrest, Gary made more than a dozen suicide attempts and, when that didn't work, resorted to alternative methods, which will be discussed later. His brother Terry was also suffering seriously by this point. He had been in and out of several mental institutions, just like Gary, and had even tried to kill himself a few times. He was unsuccessful as well.

The United Church of the Ministers of God

It took Gary a year to regroup. In October of 1971, his supremacy complex eventually took control of him, and he decided to build his own church. He incorporated a church by the name of the United Church of the Ministers of God. In the beginning, Heidnik only amassed five followers.

However, this was not an ordinary church. In a conventional church, there is not one man who has "absolute power." In Heidnik's church, he was the one who had absolute control and responsibility over all of the funds received by the church. Moreover, Heidnik also gave himself the power to veto absolutely any change in the policies of the church that were proposed by its members. He called himself the "leader for life."

It was a monolithic structure, to say the least, since all the power of the church rested with him. Heidnik originally started the church with his brother, Terry, as well as three other individuals. It was later revealed that one of the people with whom Heidnik had started the church was actually a mental patient.

They didn't have enough money to purchase a piece of land, so the United Church of the Ministers of God was formally inaugurated in a house that Heidnik owned. The house was located in the 4700 block of Cedar Avenue in West Philadelphia. He opened an account under the church's name at Merrill Lynch by making an initial deposit of $1,500. Heidnik had created a copy of the constitution of the church and had also sent it to the investment firm.

He described himself as the "church's duly elected bishop." The constitution was formally drafted, despite the fact that most of the clauses inside were heavily biased. It consisted of 18 Articles, and the most notable thing was that it declared that the office of the bishop would be held for as long as he's alive. It also said that the full "control and responsibility" of the church funds would remain with the elected bishop.

To give you a better idea about the sheer amount of control that Heidnik exercised on the church, here's a brief excerpt from Article 6 of the church's constitution: *"The duties of the bishop are many and his control extensive. . . . His is the final word on interpretation of the Bible or settling religious disputes, except for divine intervention. He will usually be able to act even without the consent or notification of the five-person board of directors."*

Again, this point links to the mentality that Heidnik shared, thinking of himself as superior to others. Even though two of the members of the church were suffering from depression and one of them was a mental patient, Heidnik still considered the need to have total control.

Many psychologists have said that Heidnik started the church just to prove to others that he was better than them. By starting a church, Heidnik was able to exercise control over his followers, and most importantly, this would be an important source of income for him, too.

Articles 12 and 13 of the church's constitution talked about dogma, stating that the guiding "inspiration" behind the church would be the Bible. However, there was severe conflict in the constitution itself. For instance, Article 12 stated that the divinity of Jesus is questionable, which is why the claim of any divine origin would not be so widely discussed in the church. It was to be "played down."

This just contradicted with the initial idea that the Church would be based on the teachings of the Bible. Article 16 listed a comprehensive number of methods in which the church was going to operate. It talked about how the donations might be utilized and how the ministers would try to spread the word. The Article was quite detailed, stating that they would try to expand the church with the "conventional technique of church building, with organs, pews and ministers, etc." The second method stated in the Article was "the much more ancient idea of small groups of individuals coming together in the home or elsewhere and praying."

Article 17 talked about making amendments to the constitution. It said that any amendments to the constitution could be made if two-thirds of the board voted for it. However, as was a recurring theme in the constitution, the bishop had the power to "irrevocably" veto the amendment if he saw fit.

It was clear that Heidnik was suffering from illusions of grandeur and that they were getting more serious by this point. By giving himself the title of bishop and bestowing all of these powers upon himself, Heidnik was now bringing his illusions into reality.

His life had suddenly found new meaning. The decision to call himself an "elected bishop" and then giving himself all of these powers simply meant that he could now exert his control and power over others. The constitution also stated that the church would not make any collections during church services. It stated that the church officers would serve and spread the "message of God" without pay. However, the constitution also stated that the money to support the church could be raised from various different sources such as stocks, bingo, loans, various business ventures, and a number of other endeavors.

Article 16 highlighted the aim of the church. It stated that "Our sacred aim is to promote the worship and teachings of God." Even though Heidnik had no intentions of doing so, the constitution did highlight how the church's funds would be divided. The last Article of the constitution, Article 18, said that "If and when dissolution should ever become necessary," it said, "the church assets should be equally divided between the Peace Corps and the Veterans Administration."

The United Church of the Ministers of God was one of the main reasons why Heidnik started calling himself Brother Heidnik. He started thinking of himself as a man who was here on a mission from God. Heidnik still believed that others were unworthy of talking to, though he soon began to realize that others didn't take kindly to him.

The mentally disabled partner in the church was the only one who treated him without any discrimination. It was easy for Heidnik to break the ice and talk to him. Moreover, it was also easy for Heidnik to manipulate mentally disabled people however he saw fit. He could beat them, scold them and push them around and there would be no retaliation.

He soon realized that mentally disabled people were easier targets. The United Church of the Ministers of God was actually a pretty lucrative venture. By the time the accounts were seized and the church was disbanded, it was found that the church had made more than $500,000. Adjusted for inflation, the amount came to around $1,079,386 in 2010. By 1986, the United Church of the Ministers of God was thriving, with almost fifty members. The church was also receiving a lot of nifty donations from anonymous donors.

It didn't take long for Heidnik to realize that his fortunes were about to make a turn for the better. In 1986, Heidnik sold his house and purchased another three-story property. Here, he rented out two of the floors and moved in with Anjeanette Davidson, who was mentally disabled. This was the time when Heidnik's fortunes began to change, and he soon started living a pretty successful life.

However, Heidnik was not very social, something the tenants were more than happy to testify to. They would usually stay out of his way for most of the time, and Heidnik would only ever meet them when it was time to collect the rent. When Heidnik was aggressive towards Anjeanette, she never spoke about it or complained to anybody.

Life of Crime

Oftentimes, serial killers go on their spree due to one reason or another. It might be a triggering event in their life, or something that went very wrong at some point in time. There's little doubt that hatred begins to boil up in their minds from a very young age.

It was the same with Heidnik. During his early years, he had been tortured mentally and physically by his father. He had been cast as a social recluse back in school. During his early years, Heidnik used to pacify himself by thinking that he was a better person than them.

Unfortunately, this was no longer an excuse. His discharge from the military and the schizoid personality disorder diagnosis was still weighing on his mind. Brother Heidnik wasn't exactly wanting for money either. The church was doing well, and he was living a pretty steady life.

It must also be known that Heidnik's sexual urges were increasing by the day. He had never been able to have sex with a woman. He wasn't exactly an affable man, and his odd-shaped head didn't really improve matters. His only sexual encounters were with his first girlfriend, Anjeanette Davidson. Heidnik later stated that he had thought sex to be something different.

In his mind, sex was going to be an "out of the world" experience. He was a serial masturbator in his childhood, and the idea of sex had always fascinated him. Unfortunately, Anjeanette didn't exactly fulfill his appetite. She was mentally disabled, and sex wasn't exactly as Gary had imagined it. This was one of the things niggling at the back of his mind for a very long time, he later revealed. He wanted the experience that others had talked about, and he had yet to experience it.

His first recorded criminal instance dates back to 1976. It was a fine, peaceful day at Heidnik's house. Gary went to the first floor and knocked. His tenant took a very long time to open, which irked Gary more. When his tenant opened the door, Gary inquired about the rent. The tenant replied that his salary had been delayed and he would pay tomorrow. Gary was quite angry and pushed the tenant in his house, demanding him to pay now.

When his client told him that he didn't

have the money and asked him to just wait a day, Gary started kicking him. An altercation ensued when his tenant pushed him away. This was the first time when Gary had ever been involved in a fight, and he didn't know how to respond. Despite the many verbal arguments he had had in the past, Gary had never been pushed around like that. This was the first time anybody had hit back, and this was no mental patient.

Enraged and not knowing what to do next, Gary knew he wasn't going to back down. It was going to leave a harsh bruise on his ego. His face was reddened with anger. In a fit of rage, Gary took out a pistol and shot the tenant at point blank range. However, his arms were trembling with rage, and the shot narrowly missed the tenant's face. The bullet just grazed his face and buried itself in the concrete wall behind him.

Gary panicked and left the floor. The sound of the shot startled the other tenants in the house. It wasn't long before an ambulance showed up, and his tenant was shifted to the hospital. Shortly thereafter, his tenant gave the official notice to leave Gary's property and also filed a lawsuit against him.

Gary was officially charged with aggravated assault. The police also found that the pistol Gary had fired was an unlicensed weapon, further compounding his misery. However, Gary was not a poor man. He was known for driving around town in expensive cars with rolls of money. It wasn't difficult for him to settle the case with his tenant, and the matter was closed. Gary was not imprisoned for his actions and continued about his life as normal.

*****

A couple of years passed with little happening. The United Church of the Ministers of God was doing well, and money was coming in. Gary was living the life of his dreams with his mentally disabled wife. In 1977, he received the news that he was going to be a father. Maxine was born in 1978, and Gary was quite happy about the birth.

However, Maxine's birth did little to change Gary's ways. In fact, it wasn't long before he began to remain perpetually angry. Anjeanette wasn't exactly able to care for her daughter, and Gary had to cut off his own activities in order to remain with the girl. He didn't exactly like that.

Gary's anger took a toll, and he decided that he would visit Anjeanette's sister, who was also a mental patient. He signed Alberta Davidson out of the institution in Harrisburg,

Pennsylvania, and brought her home. Anjeanette had tagged along with Gary to visit her sister. After he signed her out and drove her back home, Gary locked her in the basement of his house. Even though she was 34 years old, Alberta's mental age was akin to that of a toddler. Later on, when Anjeanette asked about where Alberta had gone, Gary told her that he had dropped her back at the institution.

Gary only had permission to take Alberta out for the day, since she was unable to care for herself. When she wasn't returned as per the expected time, the institution's administration called the police. A couple of days later, the police knocked on Gary's door and demanded to search the house. They found Alberta in Gary Heidnik's basement. At first sight, she seemed disheveled and was trembling with fright. Needless to say, Anjeanette was visibly shocked when her sister was brought out from her own basement. The police were suspicious about what had happened and decided that Alberta should be subjected to a full medical examination. The medical reports revealed that the poor woman had been raped and sodomized. Gary was charged with the following crimes:

- Kidnapping

- Rape
- Unlawful restraint
- False imprisonment
- Involuntary deviant sexual intercourse

He was also charged for interfering with the custody of a committed person. Gary was sentenced to seven years for his crimes at a high-security prison. However, Gary decided to appeal this because there was only one legal charge in his file, and he wasn't exactly a serial offender. The judge was very lenient and reduced his sentence to just a year and confinement in a mental institution after that.

One day in prison, Gary scribbled a note and passed it to the guard outside. Confused, the guard took it out and read it. It said that "Satan" had shoved a cookie down his throat and that Gary could no longer speak. He remained completely quiet for the next two-and-a-half years, not talking to anybody. He was released in 1983 under a state-sanctioned mental health program. He would remain in close supervision by the police during his probation time. All this while, the United Church for the Ministers of God was thriving and doing very well. Obviously, since Gary was the only one who had the authority to utilize the church's funds, he had built up a neat nest egg during his time in prison.

A year after his release, in 1984, Gary decided to shift from his current house. He sold it and bought yet another house. David Stec, one of his childhood friends, shared a basement with him. He started advertising his church in earnest, and more money began to flow in.

In 1985, Gary married again. During this time, the concept of a mail-order bride had become very popular. Gary had heard from several sources that you could browse through different options and decide which woman you wanted to marry. In exchange, all he had to do was pay a small sum of money. Betty Disto landed in Pennsylvania all the way from the Philippines. She was a good-looking, petite lady, way out of Gary's league.

However, Disto wanted stability, and Gary was a pretty stable guy when it came to finances. The two married in Maryland on the 3rd of October, 1985. However, their marriage didn't last long. One day, Disto returned home to find Gary in bed with another woman.

The couple had a huge fight. Gary eventually apologized and promised that it would never happen again. This was completely unlike

Gary. Just a few days later, Disto again found him in bed with another woman. This time when she raised her voice, Gary beat her up and forced her to watch as he had sexual intercourse with the other woman.

A few days later, Gary brought in another prostitute and forced Betty to watch him having sex with her. Needless to say, Betty filed for divorce within a few days. The two separated soon after. However, what Gary didn't know was that he had impregnated Betty. She claimed that he had repeatedly raped and assaulted her throughout their marriage.

Betty sought help from the Filipino community in Philadelphia, who helped her get away from Gary and file for her divorce. The two parted ways in January 1986. Even though Betty's role in Heidnik's life was very small, she actually left a huge impact. A year later, Betty Disto filed for child support payments, claiming that the two had conceived a son together. She named the child Jesse John Disto. Heidnik also had another baby with Gail Lincow. This child was named Gary Junior.

Because Anjeanette was unable to care for her own child, Maxine was also placed in foster care. When Betty Disto divorced Heidnik, she also decided to file criminal charges. Again, Gary Heidnik was charged with indecent assault, spousal rape, assault and involuntary deviant sexual intercourse.

However, these charges were dropped in the first hearing. When the judge asked Betty Disto to take the stand, it was found that she wasn't available. Apparently, the lady was so distressed by her experiences that she had gone into hiding with the Filipino community. As a result, the charges were dropped and Gary Heidnik was again scot-free.

*****

By this point, Gary had completely succumbed to the "demons in his head." Betty Disto had left the house soon after. After Betty's departure, Gary came up with a crazy idea that he didn't share with anyone at this point. He only talked about it much later after he was imprisoned. He had decided to start a "baby factory" in his basement. He decided to kidnap, lock up and then impregnate ten different women. He put his plan into action in November 1986.

Josefina Rivera was a prostitute who spent most of her time in North Philadelphia. Life at home wasn't exactly peaceful, since she and her boyfriend were always fighting over money. She was angry at her boyfriend for his unreasonable demands. Her boyfriend didn't like that she was a prostitute. She was an African American and making a living wasn't exactly easy, despite the fact that America had given equal rights to African Americans.

She slammed the door on her way out and left their apartment. The dingy place was located in a small slum of North Philadelphia. The night was dark, and it was pouring heavily. Despite the bitter cold and the heavy rains, Josefina walked along the road, hoping for a potential client.

Josefina Rivera

A white Cadillac Coupe DeVille slowly drove by and eventually came to a stop just a few meters ahead. Hopeful, she moved closer and leaned in the window. The man who looked back at her from the driver's seat wore glasses and a beard, and she noticed that he had a weirdly shaped head.

She asked him if he could give her a ride. The man nodded and unlocked the car. Josefina sat on the passenger's seat of the car since the man looked pretty okay to her.

Gary was carefully studying his victim. She was an African American, and he had grown up with a lot of hatred against them. Could she be the first victim? Gary didn't know what to do, so he just drove on. He introduced himself to Josefina by his name and then told her that he had to make a small stop along the way. The lady didn't mind.

Just a few minutes later, the silvery Cadillac pulled into a local McDonald's. Both Gary and Josefina got out of the car and went inside. Gary ordered coffee for himself while Josefina stayed silent. He never offered her anything. She sat across him as he sat silently and drank his coffee.

Josefina had met many men in her life, and

she always studied her potential clients before allowing them to take her home. She looked at the man sitting across from her. He was white and wore glasses. Behind the lenses, she could see piercing blue eyes staring vacantly into the mug full of black coffee. Her eyes wandered down to the hand holding the mug, and she noticed the flashy watch. It was hard to miss anyway. The watch seems expensive, she thought.

The man had a luxury car and also wore jewelry. There was a bracelet on his other wrist, and an expensive chain was wrapped around his neck. However, she was confused because his clothes seemed very cheap and were completely soiled. He didn't seem much of a talker.

Desperate to make conversation, she asked his name again. Without looking up, the man said "Gary Heidnik." Just a few minutes later, Gary looked up and told her they were leaving. He was done with his coffee. She asked him where they were headed, to which he replied that they were going to his house.

Josefina stared out the window as they entered a seedy neighborhood. The car came to a stop in front of a dilapidated, unkempt house. Josefina's keen eyes also noticed that there was a 1971 Rolls Royce parked in the driveway. She smiled to herself. Maybe she was in luck for the night; this guy sure seemed to have a good amount of money.

As they arrived at the door, Gary fished in his pockets and bought out a strange-looking key. Josefina couldn't help but notice that this was unlike any other key she had ever seen before. The lock seemed pretty normal, after all. Confused, she asked Gary about the key. He said that this was a normal lock, but he had broken the key in two, leaving half of it in the lock. This way, he said, nobody but him could enter the place.

The door gave way to a kitchen. The walls of the kitchen were adorned with pennies that had been glued to the walls. Even though Josefina had met a number of strange men in her life, many of which had different fetishes, she didn't think that Gary was going to be a problem.

The house seemed as if it hadn't been cleaned in a while. The furniture appeared aged, and it didn't seem that anybody had performed any maintenance on the house. Gary was kind and offered to show her around. As they walked through the house, Josefina couldn't believe her eyes.

She could see a hallway that had been

partially covered in one- and five-dollar bills. Given the fact that Josefina was quite poor, this was a startling sight. She had met some rich clients in the past, but none of them had ever flaunted their wealth by sticking up dollar bills on the walls.

As she was admiring the walls, two hands suddenly grabbed her throat and began to choke her. She tried to resist, and the choke loosened. However, rather than loosening his grip, Gary grabbed her arms and tied them behind her waist. He then marched her to a cold and dark basement.

Josefina Rivera was thrown on top of a dirty mattress, and metal clamps were attached to her ankles. He tied the clamps to a chain. Gary was smart, and he knew that Josefina could try and pull out of those clamps. To keep this from happening, he applied wet glue on the clamps. Then he brought out a hair dryer and dried the glue, making sure that the clamps stuck fast in their position.

The other end of the chain was fastened to a pipe running across the ceiling. By this time, Josefina had stopped screaming. She waited with bated breath to see what was going to happen. Gary seemed unfazed. He worked with methodical precision and was very calm.

After he was done tying her, he asked her to sit up. Scared and trembling, Josefina sat up. She was frightened about what he might do next. However, what happened next took her completely by surprise. He laid his head on her lap and fell asleep. It wasn't long before Josefina nodded off as well.

When she awoke during the day, she could just make out her surroundings due to the scant daylight entering from the crevices above. She soon realized the horrors of the room she was kept in. The basement had been repurposed as a prison. Right in the middle of the room, Heidnik had removed a small part of the concrete and had dug a shallow pit in the ground underneath. It wasn't long before Heidnik returned and started digging out the pit again.

While he worked, Heidnik was muttering to himself. Josefina asked why he had brought her here. He told her that all he had ever wanted was a large family. He told her that he had already fathered four children with different women. However, due to one reason or another, he had been unable to stay in touch with them.

He told Josefina that his plan was to bring ten women into the basement, impregnate them and start a family. Josefina scoffed at his plan, stating that he would never be able to succeed. Gary was enraged by her words and demonstrated his intent by raping her.

He then left the room. While she was alone, Josefina worked hard to remove her restraints. She pried open the covers from the top window and started stretching the chain until it reached to its full length. She was able to lift herself halfway out of the window. However, since she was unable to fully escape from the house, she started screaming.

To her dismay, the only person that responded to her cries was Heidnik. He brought her back down into the basement and beat her with a stick until she quieted down. He pulled Josefina in the half-dug pit in the floor, and asked her to keep her head on her chest. He then covered the top with heavy slats of wood. He also placed heavy weights atop the planks to ensure that Josefina would not be able to escape. To ensure that Josefina's cries wouldn't be heard, he also turned on a radio and put it to a heavy metal station.

Josefina stopped struggling as she realized that it wasn't going to make any difference. Her muscles went limp as she waited to die. Even as she lay silent in the pit, she could hear Gary arguing with another woman over the sound of distorted guitars. Her heart sank as she heard the sound of a chain dragging across the floor.

A little while later, the planks were lifted and much to her relief, Heidnik dragged her out from the pit. He tied Josefina to the pipe. She noticed another woman tied to the pipe in the exact same manner that she had been just one night before. The woman, oblivious to what was happening to her, was clearly in shock. She was naked except for a blouse. Josefina couldn't help but wonder why the woman remained so silent. She could see an empty look in the lady's eyes.

When Heidnik left them alone, Josefina started talking to Sandy Lindsay. It wasn't long before Josefina realized why the poor girl was so silent throughout her ordeal; she was mentally disabled. Sandy told Josefina that she had known Gary for many years.

The two had actually met when Gary was at the Elwyn Institute. She also revealed that she had sex with Gary and one of his other friends, Tony. Josefina noticed that her voice didn't even quiver as she stated her life's facts. She even spoke about how she had been impregnated and later opted for an abortion.

Josefina learned that Gary was enraged when he found out that Sandy had aborted the baby. He even offered to pay a thousand dollars to Sandy if she would have his baby. Sandy's resolve gave way as her story came to an end, realizing what a mess she was in.

The two lived in his basement as days continued to pass. One day, Heidnik came downstairs and revealed that two of Sandy's sisters had come calling, wondering if she was present at the house. Gary had turned them away. However, Gary knew that this might arouse suspicion. He asked Sandy to write a letter, explaining to her mother that she had gone away for a while and would call back later.

Gary would often come down and rape either Josefina or Sandy. He would keep them semi-naked. The two would often huddle together because the basement was very cold. They would often try to call for help, and Heidnik would beat them severely for this. He would often come up with cruel punishments.

When he thought that the two were getting used to the darkness of the pit, he came up with another cruel method. He would tie one of the lady's arms to the pipe overhead and leave them suspended for hours. Heidnik was still developing his skills as a torturer at this time.

On the other hand, Sandy's mother was actively looking for her. She told a police officer that Gary, who lived on Marshall Street, was the only person Sandy could have gone to. The officer tried calling the number several times and even visited the place a couple of times. Unfortunately, when nobody opened the door, the police officer wrote off the place.

Lisa Thomas

As Christmas approached, Gary realized that it was time to add one more "wife." He was driving around the streets at night looking for another woman when he saw a lady walking by in the night. He stopped the car beside her and made a suggestive comment to her.

Lisa was nineteen years old. She was on her way to a friend's house when the stylish Cadillac Coupe DeVille came to a stop beside her. The lewd comment put her off, and she shouted that she wasn't a prostitute. The man's tone suddenly softened, and he asked if he could give her a ride.

Lisa was startled at the sudden change in the man's behavior. He apologized immediately and said that he would even buy her a meal. He offered her a ride to Atlantic City. Lisa was surprised and accepted excitedly. Gary slipped something in her wine, and it wasn't long before she was completely unconscious.

A few hours later, Lisa awoke in a cold, damp basement with two other women. Josefina and Sandy filled Lisa in on the story, and the three women wondered how Gary would ever fit seven more women in the tiny room. All three had decided that if one of them were able to escape, they would immediately send help.

More than a week had passed, and the three women had been subjected to rape and torture on and off. One day, Gary returned from his regular nightly trips with another woman. She was to be his fourth victim. Deborah Dudley was twenty-three years old and just didn't want to go down without a fight.

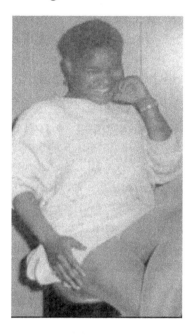

Deborah Dudley

She would question Heidnik's authority every time he would enter the room and belittle him every chance she would get. Dudley's arrival caused a bit of trouble between the other three women as well. Every time she would make a remark, not only would Gary beat her, but he would also subject the others to his beatings.

Heidnik became more and more free with his hand and started beating them quite frequently. He would often appoint one of the girls before heading out and would ask her upon return if any of the others had misbehaved. If anyone had misbehaved, he would ask the girl in charge to beat the misbehaving one.

If there was nothing to report or if Gary thought the beatings weren't severe enough, he would beat them all equally. Josefina realized that the man suffered from a superiority complex and decided to win his confidence. She started showing her loyalty and became very obedient towards Heidnik, thus giving the impression that she actually enjoyed being his wife.

The arrival of Deborah Dudley also led to a change in Heidnik's sexual appetite. He would now rape all of the women on a regular basis. Apart from having sex with all of them regularly, he would also demand that they have sex with each other while he watched. He provided a portable toilet to the women and gave them baby wipes to clean themselves.

A while later, the girls were even allowed

to have a shower, after which he would submit them to sex. Gary had still not resolved the issue of food. Some days, the girls would only receive water and bread. Other days, he would give them Philly steak sandwiches!

However, this problem was resolved when Gary decided to feed them only canned dog food. When they would refuse, Gary would beat them until they would clean their plates. A few days later, he returned with another woman, Jacquelyn Askins. She was eighteen years old.

Jacquelyn Askins

Gary raped her several times before bringing her down in the basement. When he discovered that she couldn't be tied properly to the shackles since her ankles were too small, he opted for handcuffs. He also brought Chinese food later in the day in order to celebrate Josefina's birthday. She was fast becoming his favorite "wife."

Heidnik was under the impression that Sandy and Josefina had become pregnant, and he was in a very good mood. With the passage of time, Gary's torture methods and beatings became more and more severe. In February of 1987, Gary punished Sandy for trying to lift the planks off the pit. He hung her from a roof beam by handcuffing one of her wrists, and left her there for several days.

Her condition deteriorated very quickly, and she eventually refused to eat. She was running a high fever as well. Gary, thinking that she was faking it, beat her up, dragged her down and put her in the basement. He served ice cream to the others. Throughout the week, Gary tried to force feed Sandy by pushing food in her mouth and holding it closed until she swallowed.

One day, he returned and took Sandy's limp body from the pit. He checked for a pulse and didn't find any. He told the others that she had probably choked on the food and carried her body upstairs. The other girls were shocked. Their shock soon turned into horror when they heard a power saw whirring to life.

Shock and horror turned into genuine fear when just a little while later, Gary's dog came downstairs with a big, meaty bone and ate it in front of the women. Investigators later found out that Gary had chopped Lindsay's flesh with a meat processor and then fed it to the dogs. Even the captives were fed the meat as Gary mixed it with dog food and forced the others to eat it. He cooked what was left of Sandy on the stove to dispose of it.

It wasn't long before a very foul stench filled up the house. It got so bad that the neighbors complained. A policeman arrived at Gary's doorstep to investigate. Gary assured the policeman that it was from an overcooked roast dinner and nothing else. Sandy's death was a problem for Gary to deal with, and his behavior soon turned quite bizarre.

He would ask the girls to inform on one another and promised better conditions for those who complied. The girls thought that they would attack him one day. Unfortunately, they could never carry out this plan. Later on, investigators were told by Jacqueline that Josefina had told Heidnik of their plan.

He then started coming up with more heinous ways to torture the women. He would tie them with one hand to the ceiling and leave them hanging with blindfolds covering their eyes. He would also gag them. Heidnik was convinced that the girls were constantly plotting against him. He then took a screwdriver and tried to gouge it in their ears to try to deafen them. However, Josefina was exempted from this punishment. After all, if they couldn't hear him coming, they wouldn't be able to do anything.

Deborah became increasingly defiant during this time. One day, Heidnik took her upstairs for a little while. When she returned, Deborah was completely silent. The others asked about what had happened. Deborah replied that Gary had shown her a pot inside which was Sandy Lindsay's head. He also had an oven where Sandy's ribcage was being roasted. His fridge had various other body parts, such as her arm and legs, wrapped in plastic.

It took Deborah several days to recover from what she had seen. However, she soon regained her composure and started mocking

Heidnik again. Heidnik then came up with a cruel new trick to try to silence the girls. He removed the insulation from a naked wire, plugged it in a socket and would hold the bare wire against their chains, watching with pleasure as the girls squirmed in pain.

Again, Josefina was exempted from this torture. He then came up with a new method of torturing the girls. He filled the pit in the ground with water, and pushed all three girls in the water. He even enlisted Josefina's help. As the women sat inside the pit, shivering, they noticed the bare wire touching the water, sending a jolt of electricity through them.

The wire then made direct contact with Deborah's chain. She screamed uncontrollably, and collapsed to the floor. Jacqueline and Lisa continued to shout until he removed the planks. Confirming that Deborah was dead, Gary proceeded to make sandwiches. While the women sobbed uncontrollably, Gary's demeanor was quite calm. He told them that they should be glad it wasn't one of them.

He then brought out a pen and paper and asked Josefina to write about her participation in Deborah's death. In case she ever went to the cops, he would use this as insurance that she had also helped. Josefina didn't mind at all. Gary was completely convinced that she was on his side. He then asked her to go up and change. For the first time in four months, Josefina Rivera was fully dressed.

He then wrapped Deborah's body in plastic and kept it in a freezer. Josefina became his confidante. She would constantly accompany him to various outings and the two would go out to restaurants. One day, Gary told her that he had been fooling the authorities for many years, and if he ever got caught, he would just tell the authorities that he was insane. He said that he knew how to fool the tests as well.

After Deborah's death, Heidnik also softened considerably. He provided blankets and mattresses, and even a television set to the other women. One day, the two were passing through the woods when Heidnik stopped the car and decided that it would be a good place to hide Dudley's body. The following night, the pair put Dudley's body in the car. While Josefina waited, Gary took the body and dumped it in the woods.

Gary then told Josefina that he needed to find a replacement for Dudley. He enlisted Josefina's help in trapping his next victim, Agnes Adams. As soon as they arrived at the house,

Agnes found herself stripped and chained with other women in the basement. Gary didn't even suspect that Josefina might have other plans.

Agnes Adams

On the 24th of March, Josefina finally

succeeded. She had been trying to convince Gary for a long while to allow her to visit her family. She told him that she would return with another "wife" if he let her go, thus allowing him to expand his family. Excited at the prospect, Gary relented. She asked Gary to pick her up from the nearby station in the night. As soon as Heidnik dropped her off, Josefina ran over to her apartment and told her story to her boyfriend, Vincent Nelson.

For a while, Nelson thought that she had gone crazy. Here was a woman he hadn't seen for the past four months, standing on his doorstep, recounting tales of dogs eating human flesh, cannibalism and hideous tales of torture. She then called the police and recounted her story to the police. Even the policemen didn't believe her until she showed them the bruises made by the chains on her ankles.

The policemen, David Savidge and John Cannon, decided to go with Josefina. They approached the white Coupe DeVille. Heidnik raised his arms in the air, asking the policemen if they were there to ask about his child support payments. He had been fooling the authorities for a long while, showing himself to be mentally ill. However, the policemen waved off his claims, and asked him to raise his hands up in the air. His reign of terror was finally over.

The Cellar of Death

Just before the clock struck 5:00 a.m. on the morning of March 25[th,] 1987, Homicide Lieutenant James Hansen and a squad of police cars stopped in front of 3520 North Marshall Street. When they couldn't break down the door due to his intricate lock system, Hansen asked his officers to break down the door.

Office David Savidge, along with Officer McCloskey, headed straight for the basement under the directions given by Josefina. As Savidge's eyes readjusted to the dark, damp environment, he could make out the shape of two women lying on a small mattress. The two women started to scream as the officers approached them. He reassured them that he was a police officer and was only there to save them.

David noticed that the women weren't wearing anything except socks and thin blouses. David asked if there were other women in the house. Both the ladies pointed to the planks on the floor. The officers removed the dirt bags and moved the planks. The sight of Agnes squatting in the pit greeted their eyes.

The officers lifted her out and took all of the women upstairs to an ambulance. Now that the women were free, the officers focused their attention on searching the house. They found an aluminum pot with a lot of burn marks on it. There was a yellowish fatty substance inside. They found an industrial food processor that had recently been used. They found human ribs and body parts in the freezer.

Officer David Savidge couldn't believe what he had been seeing. Over the course of several days, police searched each and every part of the house. They found a closet full of pornographic material, exclusively featuring black women. They bagged everything they could find so that it could later be used as evidence.

Police digging out basement where he tortured, raped and killed.

Terry Heidnik (brother)

Michael Heidnik (father)

*Back of the house at
3520 North Marshall Street, Philadelphia*

The Trial

In Custody 1987

On the 23rd of April, 1987, Gary Michael Heidnik was served up in court. Alongside him sat his counsel, Charles Peruto. Peruto had a reputation for defending sensational cases. He was a sharp-minded defense attorney. Heidnik was formally charged with the following:

- Murder

- Kidnapping
- Rape
- Involuntary deviant sexual intercourse
- Aggravated assault
- False imprisonment
- Indecent exposure
- Simple assault
- Indecent assault
- Unlawful restraint and various other offences.

Perhaps the most damning form of evidence against Heidnik was the testimony given by the captives. The first witness to take the stand was Lisa, who described in clear detail how Heidnik had chained her and beaten her. The next to take the stage was Josefina. She was clear and confident as she explained her whole ordeal, highlighting the murders of Sandy Lindsay and Deborah Dudley. She also clearly stated that it was her who had pushed the wire in the pit.

Lisa blamed Josefina, stating that she accompanied Heidnik and helped him torture the women. However, Jacqueline clarified that Josefina only punished them when she was being threatened by Heidnik himself. The last person to take the stand was Dr. Paul Hoyer from the county medical examiner's office.

He brought with him a list of all the evidence that had been recovered. The court room fell silent as the doctor started reading the pieces of evidence procured from Heidnik's house: two forearms, two knees, segments of thighs, an upper arm and various other body parts, including muscle tissue and skin. In total, more than twenty-four pounds of human remains were found in Heidnik's house. Within minutes, Gary Heidnik had been indicted and was slated for trial.

The trial started on the 20th of June, 1988. Heidnik was presented in a packed courtroom. As soon as the trial began, Charles Gallagher, the prosecutor, started bringing witnesses to the stand. For two days, the jury of six blacks and six whites listened to the gruesome details.

At one point in time, Peruto argued that the charge of first degree murder should be dropped. He stated that because the grounds for intent to kill had not been established, first-degree murder could not stand. However, Judge Lynne Abraham replied with one word, "overruled."

Peruto's whole defense was based on the testimony of two men, Dr. Clancy McKenzie and psychologist Jack Apsche. However, Peruto didn't know that McKenzie had something else in mind. When he took the stand, McKenzie started talking about schizophrenia and other mental conditions. His intellectual statements left the jury more confused, thus damaging Heidnik's case even further.

Eventually, Peruto asked him whether Heidnik knew the difference between right and wrong, to which he replied in the negative. Peruto then focused on Josefina, asking the jury to consider the possibility that she might actually have been an accomplice.

The Judge agreed that she would let the jury consider the possibility, if it meant that Peruto would accept that Heidnik was capable of enlisting the aid of an accomplice, clearly the act of a sane man. The next day, most of Apsche's testimony was rendered inadmissible by Abraham.

In a desperate attempt to prove his point, Peruto called another psychiatrist to the stand. This time it was Dr. Kenneth Kool. Even though Kool gave his professional opinion on Heidnik's mental health, the judge didn't accept most of it.

Dr. Kenneth further damaged his own testimony by admitting that he had just spent twenty minutes with Heidnik and then had left in frustration.

Charles Gallagher knew that the case was an open and close. However, to add insult to injury, he called Robert Kirkpatrick to the stand. Mr. Kirkpatrick was a broker at Merrill Lynch with whom Gary had worked while opening the United Church of the Ministers of God. Robert clearly told the jury that Heidnik was an astute investor and knew exactly what he was doing. Even so, Peruto was confident that Heidnik might not be convicted for first degree murder and thus might escape the death penalty.

The jury deliberated for more than sixteen hours before passing on their verdict to the judge. On the 30th of June, 1988, Judge Abraham stood up in anticipation of the jury spokesperson's verdict that sealed Heidnik's fate. Chuck Bennett, the spokesperson for the jury, knew what had been decided, and his words were clear. "For the murder of Deborah Dudley, guilty in the first degree. For the murder of Sandra Lindsay, guilty in the first degree."

The courtroom fell completely silent as the list went on. By the time Bennett fell silent, Gary

Michael Heidnik had been convicted on more than eighteen charges. The jury was dismissed at 9:00 am the following day. Within a few hours, the jury had decided on the death penalty for Gary Heidnik. Throughout the course of the trial itself, Gary had remained relatively quiet. Gary remained completely silent and showed no emotion whatsoever when the sentence was read out.

In January 1989, Gary Heidnik tried to commit suicide by overdosing on thorazine. Yet again, he failed. Ten years passed as Heidnik languished in jail, waiting for the day when he would be put to his death. In 1997, Maxine Davidson White, his daughter, and Betty Heidnik, his ex-wife, tried to file for a stay of execution.

They stated that Heidnik was not competent enough for execution. This came as a surprise to most, since he had been declared competent for execution just two days before.

However, Heidnik was not a party to the action, and he repeatedly asked the court to forgo any proceedings since that might just delay the execution. Both Betty and Maxine fought to delay the execution for the next two years, but to little avail. They argued before a panel of three judges at the United States Court of Appeals for the Third Circuit. However, their appeals meant little, and on the 3rd of July, 1998, the United States District Court for the Eastern District of Pennsylvania gave its final ruling, denying White's application for a stay of execution. The petition for Writ of Habeas Corpus was also declined, and the Court also denied the certificate of appealability.

Execution

The execution warrant had already been signed by the Governor of Pennsylvania,, and Gary Michael Heidnik's death was scheduled for July 6, 1999. The final ruling by the court effectively ended any sort of recourse. On the 6th of July, the officials carried Gary Heidnik to the death chamber. He showed little or no emotion. A lethal injection was administered, and he soon succumbed to his death. As of this year, Gary Heidnik was the last person to be executed by lethal injection by the State of Pennsylvania.

A psychological evaluation had called him "psycho-sexually" immature. Gary Heidnik was known by the locals as the city's "most dysfunctional citizen." He was one of the most notorious criminals America had ever seen, and the four months of torture that he had carried out on the women will long be remembered.

His father was 74 years old when he found out about his son's actions. He had once been a councilman himself and had disowned his son many years before. When he found out about Gary's actions, he gave a stern judgment for his own son, stating that he ought to be hanged.

Four sisters of Sandy Lindsay and Deborah Dudley were present at the execution. They wore all white clothes. When Heidnik was pronounced dead at 10:29 p.m., one of them exclaimed, "Thank you, Jesus." Kathy Swedlow was one of the lawyers that Maxine had hired to delay her father's execution. Swedlow was disappointed at the execution, stating that the State had executed a mentally challenged and incompetent man.

The department released a formal statement, saying that the execution was carried out just as planned. Gary had offered no last statements and showed no resistance at all. Witnesses present at the scene described how the execution was carried out. They said a grey person opened the curtains at 10:18 p.m., showing the prisoner strapped to a gurney. He was completely silent.

An intravenous line leading into another room was inserted into his arm. The only movement was the movement of his chest as he breathed. He didn't move any muscle as the drugs moved through his system. Finally, his chest fell, and his lips parted as Heidnik took his last breath. Within ten minutes, Heidnik was dead. Despite the fact that Heidnik's case had been controversial from the start, judgment was swift. Heidnik's name will go down in history as being one of the most gruesome killers America had ever seen, and he became the 555th person to be executed in the United States of America.

Other Books By RJ Parker

Experience a thought-provoking and engrossing read with books from RJ Parker Publishing. Featuring the work of crime writer and publisher RJ Parker, as well as many other authors, our company features exciting True CRIME and CRIME Fiction books in eBook, Paperback, and Audiobook editions.

rjpp.ca/RJ-PARKER-BOOKS

Serial Killers Encyclopedia

The ultimate reference for anyone compelled by the pathology and twisted minds behind the most disturbing of homicidal monsters. From A to Z, and from around the world, these serial killers have killed in excess of 3,000 innocent victims, affecting thousands of friends and family members. There are monsters in this book that you may not have heard of, but you won't forget them after reading their case. This reference book will make a great collection for true crime aficionados.

WARNING: *There are 15 dramatic crime scene photos in this book that some may find extremely disturbing*

Amazon Links- *eBook* | *Paperback* | *Audiobook*

This collection of "Filicidal Killers" provides a gripping overview of how things can go horribly wrong in once-loving families. Parents Who Killed their Children depicts ten of the most notorious and horrific cases of homicidal parental units out of control. People like Andrea Yates, Diane Downs, Susan Smith, and Jeffrey MacDonald who received a great deal of media attention. The author explores the reasons, from addiction to postpartum psychosis, insanity to altruism, revenge and jealousy. Each story is detailed with background information on the parents, the murder scenes, trials, sentencing and aftermath.

SUSPENSE MAGAZINE - *"Parents Who Kill Their Children is a great read for aficionados of true crime. The way the author laid the cases out made the hair on the back of my neck stand up."*

Amazon Links- *eBook | Paperback | Audiobook*

Thank you to my editor, proofreaders, and cover artist for your support:

~ RJ

Aeternum Designs (book cover)

Bettye McKee (editor)

Lee Knieper Husemann

Lorrie Suzanne Phillippe

Marlene Fabregas

Darlene Horn

Ron Steed

Katherine McCarthy

Robyn MacEachern

Kathi Garcia

Linda H. Bergeron

About the Author

RJ Parker, Ph.D. is an award-winning and bestselling true crime author and owner of RJ Parker Publishing, Inc. He has written over 20 true crime books which are available in eBook, paperback and audiobook editions, and have sold in over 100 countries. He holds certifications in Serial Crime, Criminal Profiling and a PhD in Criminology.

To date, RJ has donated over 3,000

autographed books to allied troops serving overseas and to our wounded warriors recovering in Naval and Army hospitals all over the world. He also donates to Victims of Violent Crimes Canada.

If you are a police officer, firefighter, paramedic or serve in the military, active or retired, RJ gives his eBooks freely in appreciation for your service.

Contact Information

Author's Email:

AuthorRJParker@gmail.com

Publisher's Email:

Agent@RJParkerPublishing.com

Website:

http://m.RJPARKERPUBLISHING.com/

Twitter:

http://www.Twitter.com/realRJParker

Facebook:

https://www.Facebook.com/AuthorRJParker

Amazon Author's Page:

rjpp.ca/RJ-PARKER-BOOKS

** SIGN UP FOR OUR MONTLY NEWSLETTER **

http://rjpp.ca/RJ-PARKER-NEWSLETTER

References

1. http://murderpedia.org/male.H/h1/heidnik-gary.htm

2. http://criminalminds.wikia.com/wiki/Gary_He idnik

3. http://content.time.com/time/magazine/article/ 0,9171,963945,00.html

4. http://truecrimecases.blogspot.ca/2012/08/gar y-heidnik.html

5. http://www.crimezzz.net/serialkillers/H/HEID NIK_gary.php

6. http://www.crimeandinvestigation.co.uk/show s/videos/serial-killer-profile-gary-heidnik

7. http://www.executedtoday.com/2014/07/06/19 99-gary-heidnik-serial-kidnapper/

8. https://www.youtube.com/watch? v=jQh0KAiJD-A (Survivor tells her story)